if nothing else

Harold Bowes

Some of these poems appeared previously in the following magazines: *Acorn, American Tanka, Black Bough, Eleven Bulls, elimae, Failbetter, Heron's Nest, Lynx, Magazine of Speculative Poetry, Mayfly, Pig Iron Malt, Raw Nervz, Reflections, Snow Monkey, Taint, Tinywords*, and *Wind Chimes.*

Cover Artist: Bob Dornberg
http://www.dornberg-impressionism.com/

SECOND EDITION

ISBN: 978-0-9851520-7-9

Published by Ravenna Press
Spokane, Washington   USA

(continued from the back cover)

From Neil Leadbeater's review:

...the theme of transience and the celebration of the fleeting moment that recurs in the text.

...it pulls us in like a zoom lens from the general to the specific....a subtlety that is pursued with refined professionalism in the text.

Harold Bowes is a skilled practitioner in the art of the small poem.

Many of the poems in this book, it seems to me, celebrate the moment. Like a photograph taken on a whim, they pin down something that is at once very ordinary but also extraordinarily beautiful.

The strength of many of the short poems in

which a single thought or several thoughts interconnect.

There is always this journey from one place to another ...this moving imagery that never stays still yet is caught on camera in the mind.

From Tony Telschow's review:

if nothing else seems like a sustained showcase of the mind of man in middle age.

...a mood of disciplined placidity is maintained.

I would say that his modest but real achievement is the consistent presentation of a "still point at the center" sensibility, with its hints of recoil and resolution. This sensibility is sustained through the book's 58 short pages, and Bowes's craft seems evident in the selection.

Contents

if nothing else
there are these clouds
floating away

Yin

The world we live in is but thickened light.
                                    - Emerson

In the sand dollar,
there's a hole,
right in the middle.
Something lived inside,
then it was gone.
The space filled
with salt water.

What a beautiful shape,
round like the moon,
narrow along the perimeter,
then, like thickened light,
rising toward the center.

2

The air entered here
through this small hole.
Everything dried out.
The air was both inside
and outside.

Stippled and curved,
there's a design.

haloed moon —
in the dark field water spills
from a silver pipe

*

haloed moon —
she walks through shadow bringing
wood for the fire

4

cloud

Concrete Turtle

I washed my car today for the
first time this new spring.

A statement affirming love
written in the dust
which had seemed permanent through the
   winter
came away easily.

When I stood I noticed someone had
left the tub from inside a washing machine
on my front lawn.
The matted imprint would be there awhile.

Neighbors argued.
Crows cawed.
The sun had a long, hard edge to it.

The concrete turtle you gave
me and which I put on my
front stairs continues to startle me.
For such a long time there was nothing there,
now a turtle,
and from a distance sometimes
I can't make it out and wonder,
what's that,
or leaving the house
for the first time in the morning,
when I see it, I start, step back.

Light was everywhere today,
bright in the hose water,
and I got tired
and I went back inside.

the dark yard--
a few grass blades
hold the moonlight

*

a bean plant growing
in a place without light—
her long white fingers

The Night Has Murdered

The night has murdered
a summer day.
It was an effort.
It took a long time.
The stars are like beads of sweat.

My Daughter Draws

My daughter draws
Chalk faces on the sidewalk
Each with two eyes and a mouth
Heads shaped like tombstones
Like bells

House on an Upward Sloping Lot

We walk up a flight of stairs,
then up again, through the front door and inside
where Karen takes my jacket.
I almost call her Kim, then change to Karen,
but speak under my breath in case I'm wrong.
We mingle in the unfurnished living room,
try to walk out onto the patio
but can't get the door open,
go downstairs, where we run into
a couple I should know, and we talk with them
    about the remodel,
and I glance at a stairwell going down another
    level.
We wander into a bare bedroom and while you
    keep watch
I step into an empty walk-in closet to tuck in my
    shirt.
You explain my connection to the couple,
then we're back upstairs and
this time you figure out the patio door,

10

which sticks and may be the only thing not
    replaced in the remodel,
and we're out into the back yard,
to see the terraces that climb up behind the
    house,
and talk to another couple, and the women
    knows who I am,
but I don't know who she is,
then inside again, over to the buffet
where I ask you the names of the different
    dishes.
We fill a paper plate and retreat to an empty
    bedroom,
sit in folding chairs, and talk about our Japanese
    exchange student,
whose name I can't remember so I call her
"our Japanese exchange student" and we finish
    eating
and walk through the hallway and out into the
    night.

I knew I would forget my jacket.

Her name was Erika.

Banking

From the plane
how small the river appears,
even as sunlight glitters across it.
We were not meant to be
in this place.

In the Mirror

The light comes in
from the hallway
and in the mirror on the wall
to the left of the bed
I can see another wall
and a piece of the curtain
and other things.

They all look shinier
than they really are.

Because I hurt her,
though not intending to,
she needs to hurt me and does.

The wrinkles on your knuckles
and up there by your fingernails,
I guess those are the wrinkles that
you are born with.

Like

Like the way sometimes
The nail is visible above the frame and
The wire that holds the painting to the wall
Outlines a low lying hill or
When you straighten the painting
A shape shifting sand dune
Like the way sometimes
The nail holds a calendar to the wall
The calendar displaying a black and white
photograph
Of a canyon with the full moon high in the
  sky
The nail hole is so big, so big,
You can see the wall through it
Like the way the wall is painted white
Like a second moon
The nail head like a partial eclipse

Riding in a Car

It's the summer
And you've been reading
As the car goes from point a to point b
Someone else driving
When there's a brief soundless rain shower
You look up
The wet pavement suddenly black
It's wonderful
Like walking laps at the health club
When the blood starts to rush
That warmth

Our Car

Our car paces a truck.
The truck is hauling
detached automobile bumpers,
secured to a flatbed.
The mountains are white with snow
in the distance.
The clouds are as big as Montana.
Even now I forgive you.

clouds

Columbia River Gorge

The moss covered monoliths.

We are on our way to The Dalles.
I am the passenger this time.

Where the old highway parallels the freeway
it runs along the ridgeline higher up.
Sometimes we see antique bridges
made of white concrete.

The snow is melting.

Waterfalls cascade down a cliff face.
The rain is coming down too.

We see five rainbows.

Within its pale bands
along its narrow length

18

there is such stillness
in the rainbow,

and so much motion,
such an absence of color
in the waterfall.

As we move along
the long black highway
I drift into sleep

and everything changes.

Evening Light

Our fifth-wheel looks completely different
in the evening light: three dimensional,
and banded in shadow. I'm glad that
we came out here to talk.
We talk about what we would do
if we had the winning Powerball ticket,
how we would funnel the 280 million dollars
into charitable trusts and put your father
and mother, my brothers and sisters,
on their boards and payrolls, and,
as we look out over fields to the horizon,
the clouds start to turn a rose color.
Standing here in the half light,
we talk about how far we have come
and how far we have to go,
where we were yesterday,
where we will be tomorrow,
and as we talk the lights in the trailer court,
the one next door to this campground

that we're parked in, start coming on.
While you massage my back, and,
as the rose tint is leaving the clouds,
I begin to think that we will make it.
Out a quarter mile I can see
the wind moving through
the darkened leaves in a cottonwood,
its bark as white as hope
in the dim sunlight.

all around
the parking meter
spring rain!

*

spring sky
a toddler walks outside
in a blue cowboy suit

*

summer moon—
dangling on her sleeve
a silver button

*

summer birds—
the rise of our baby's chest
against mine

22

summer drought—
next to her rose tattoo
a pale blue vein

*

where the stem ends
there should be something bright,
a flower, some fruit,
where your arm narrows, there is this:
your hand, the unadorned fingers

*

dark winter morning—
on her neck a white thread
through clear glass beads

*

rising through
the ginkgo's bare limbs—
a smoke plume

23

Memoir in Seven Parts

1.

lamp light
in a room
open to the night
I tell you everything
about myself

2.

his head way up there
almost touching the car's roof
dad drives deep
into the interior

3.

I don't remember
one thing you bought there

a sheet of S&H green stamps
would have fit right inside the frame
of this photo of you

4.

that a river would bend
it's nearly too much to think about
I live where the river bends
out in the yard my child
bouncing on a trampoline

5.

the way paint
on old construction equipment
dulls but stays
what can I say?
I love you

6.

deepest winter
opening the medicine cabinet
my hand in the mirror
gets larger
still larger

7.

I have nothing to say
"It's quiet"
I will say that
and somewhere sunlight
is flashing on water

Migration

On its migration north
the HOLLYWOOD sign lost an "L",
like a biplane might lose a wing.
It came to rest on a hillside above Lewiston,
Idaho
If you live there then, during the night,
after watching a movie or a television program
you dream of falling.
In your dream, you grasp onto
hundreds of useless feathers
so desperately, in either hand.

I Ask the Clerk

I ask the clerk
the name of the river.
"Clearwater," she says.
I don't ask about the small
blue birds with black crests.

the clouds

In a Black Train, Tokyo

The train I am riding accelerates
past a train on a parallel track,
gaining, but slowly,
which gives me time to study
the faces in the windows
of the other train:

heartbreakingly beautiful
young Japanese faces,
with blank expressions.

It is the feeling you have
while standing in a train
looking out through a window,
when your mind is
turned inward
and yet you feel the most
connected to society.

You are often alone

when this happens.
You feel you are the
reason for the train.

You want someone to
see you and admire you
(I am that someone today).
You feel you are beautiful
or in a state of beauty.

In Niiza City this morning
I heard a raven's cry
echo between buildings

I remember a time
in the detached palace garden
feeding small dried fish
to the feral cats while
ravens waited in the trees.

I imagine a place
in a pine grove far away,
deep in a dark green shadow

where ravens glide
from branch to branch.

Our train slows
and the faces in the other train
reappear but moving faster
and in the opposite order.
I remember them all
as though I know them
from somewhere else,
but with increasing speed
the faces blur,
the memory is lost.

Moving across my inner eyelids:
the lines of red paper lanterns at Asakusa,
bright silver Pachinko balls falling, falling.

Sometimes the light follows
around the edge of the window
making a white place.
My thoughts are
in that place now.

Looking Through a Telescope

It would be like looking into a dark room
A man would be holding a small, white
    flower
But you would not see the man, nor the stem
only the flower, and there would be a breeze,
a window open, and the petals would flicker
It would be as though the man had stood,
the
flower would be very high, he was a tall man
You knew this, and it would be this way every
    night
every night that the door would be open

trimming the white
borders from her nails
radiant morning light
from every window
in the house

*

sheet-draped window
through the folds and creases
a bright moon
turning away—
your narrow back

*

all the brushstrokes
on the bedroom door
going down
I wait for
her answer

34

when I put
the tanka zine on the ledge
next to the tomato
my wife takes it and slices it
into many pieces

                *

leaving…
far down this street
how bright the neon
in a place
I will never be

                *

weaving down
the tree-lined street
in a bright yellow taxi
its back seat crowded
with balloons

Object

I don't know why I'm here
or here. We moved here and
my family helped. My favorite
aunt drove my red '67 Camaro.
We came from the coast and
now we're here. The brown
hills, the rivers dry in summer,
the lack of rain, the snow in
winter, the time between.
When you have a keepsake,
as long as you keep something,
the memory, the memory stays new.
I sold the Camaro today.

some clouds

Cruise

At dinner, a retired woman says
"I worked there eight years." She says,
"One year at the company talent show
I told them, please don't announce me.
I don't want to sing if I'm nervous.
But I did sing and they said,
'There, that's our Delores.'"

After dinner, my wife and I leave
and go to the lounge to have tea.
The lemon in her cup sinks
under the weight of sugar,
but as the sugar dissolves,
the yellow slice resurfaces,
like a little sun.

Ashore we find
a hermit crab
the size of an earwig

inside a shell shaped
like the point on
a sharpened pencil.

Farther down the beach
the kiosk at the snorkeling place
is painted blue, pink, yellow, green and
   purple,
with a few spilled drops of paint
that had dried on the unpainted deck,
the walls behind not painted at all.

Back in our cabin
her bare features relaxed, completely relaxed,
there is still this one line on her forehead
and wrinkles at the corners of her mouth.

The next morning
when I cut my fingernails
a small pain persists in each nail
for a few minutes afterward.

When we return to port

we go buy sea shells at the shell shop,
take them to the ocean and toss them in.

Somewhere on a far off pacific shore
there is a cold beach with gray sand
where, at the tideline, black stones dry
briefly to a pale robin's egg blue.

peeling the egg
the skin comes away
with the shell

*

after new paint—
shadow of the coat hook
on the bedroom door

*

the rectangular chimneys
on the houses against the bay:
doors in a (white) wall

Dream, Dream, Dream, Dream

I'm far out in a great expanse of water and
my wedding ring keeps almost slipping off.
My wife is there, somehow, so I'm afraid or
    maybe
she isn't but I'm afraid I will have to explain
    its loss to her later.
I swim in place for a while and manage to tie
    the ring
to the cinch cord that goes around my
    swimming trunks.
Then I'm swimming and swimming never
    certain
if the ring is still there and I'm so worried I
    forget all about the wife.
I'm far out in a great expanse of water and
my wedding ring keeps almost slipping off.
My wife is there, somehow, so I'm afraid or
    maybe

Company

When the company leaves,
while they keep us in their memories,
things take on an added significance
as we go about our lives.
The light is brighter,
objects stand out
starkly against one another,
and the brightly hued paint on buildings
stings our eyes.
For a while we feel like characters in a novel.
For a time there is a plot,
a reason for this.

Farm Sky

Where palm
and finger
join I see

a deflated
blister the
harvest

moon. In
summer I
lift

irrigation
pipe
reassemble

the line
the horizon.
I press

a vein
flat the
sky close.

44

these clouds

Aerial Photographs

a farmer is proud
proud of his farm
so when someone comes
comes with a large framed photograph
of his farm
taken from the air
so few people come to his door
then to come with a photograph
of his farm
and framed
he listens
you listen
this is something he can buy
that will make his farm immortal
immortal on his farmhouse wall
the living room wall
immortal
there was the one my father bought
but it was a little different then

the photograph was in black and white
and someone painted colors in later

yes, it was a painting
a painting of your farm
and as paintings are
maybe a little better
than the reality
the disused field
behind the barn
now painted pasture green
and the weeds in the orchard
they disappeared
but this happened:

the concrete floor was going in
going in the new shop building
my father takes me
takes me and my brothers
and while the concrete is still wet
has us put our feet in
and leave a depression

he writes the date
in the painting the shop
covered with silver tin
is bright like a brilliant light
a brilliant light
an emptiness that comes
comes with the tingle at the end of my nerves
something I have made
something that is lost
I will keep going this way

printed in black ink
on a folded white paper napkin
"KAYAK"

　　　　*

on all of my hand
only this one small
speck of ink

　　　　*

going outside with
tea in a paper cup
at the end of the tea bag string
a green paper square
lifts in the breeze

grocery list:
white bread, white rice,
light bulbs

*

shadow of this coat hook
now the shadow of my jacket

*

business trip ending
my shadow pulls a brief case
from the car trunk

50

autumn river—
pulled together on the deck
two white chairs

      *

in the wheelbarrow
   patches of rust
   filled with frost

      *

conversation lags—
far out on the spindly beach
a withered leaf

fallen leaves
settle deeper—
the hammock's sag

*

flying into the wind
pausing,
this comma,
this ink black crow

*

loud music
coming from the tavern
back at the hotel
there is nothing to put on
that will make me look young

The Distance of Light

There is a discomfort associated with
the blackness that is the housefly, a darting
  blackness.
There is a discomfort associated with
the blackness that is the darkness, in corners
and high spaces, but the night sky is a
  comfort.
There is a sheen like rock there, there is a
  sheen
and, as though fossils imbedded,
there is the light.

Road and Parking Lot

Light from the dashboard
sifts through the car's dark interior.

Through the windshield we watch
as headlights illuminate asphalt,

as above I know there are stars
that brighten the night.

The next morning
in the motel parking lot,

you stand for a while looking at
all of the trees,

black oak, willow, apple, pine,
in a nearby field together,

green on shade of green,
tops fused into a ragged line.

On the other side of this poem
is a receipt for fuel.

54

winter stars—
shaking rust down from
the old swing set

*

morning light…
the curtain edges
darken

*

new year—
a thin layer of rainwater
coats the window

*

crescent moon—
from below so much water
a narrow stem bends

deep in the woods
all the shadows bend
toward home

       mori fukashi
       kage mina tawami
       ie wo sasu

    *

just to know
that it is orange
inside this cantaloupe
is enough
for now

Before

The wind
streaked
the lawn

a lighter
green. A
bee a

fingernail
tapped my
window. A

blue jay
carried an
acorn in

its beak.
Now
clouds.

The valley
a canoe
narrows

toward the
end here.